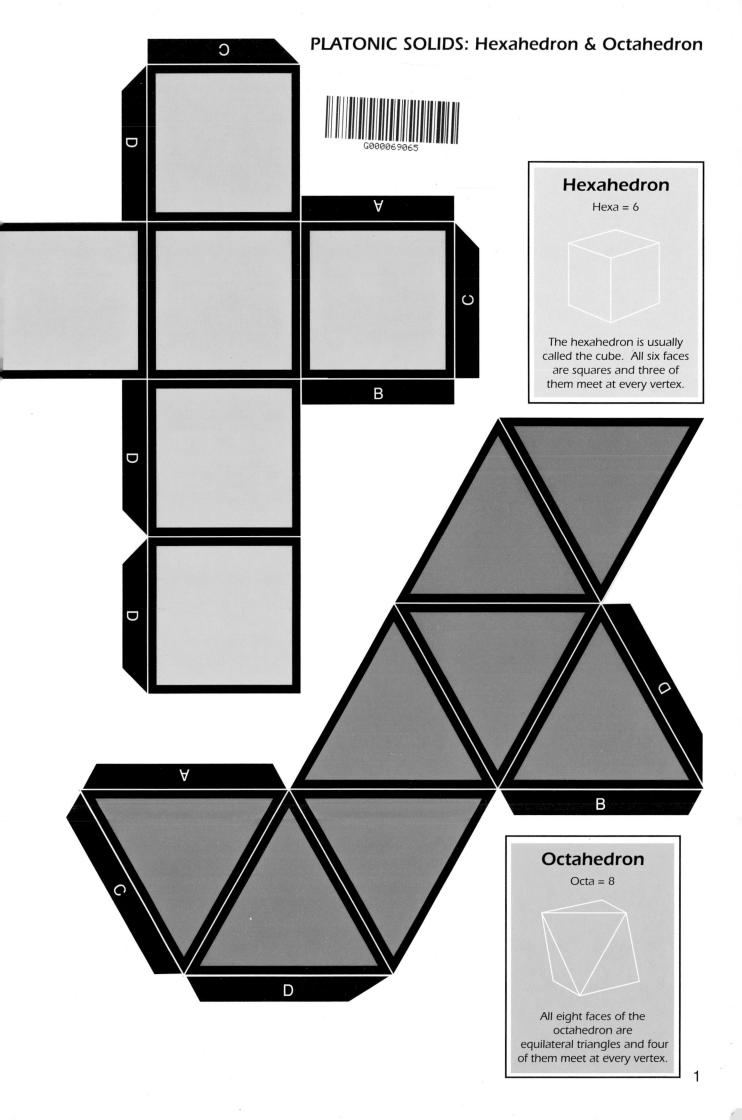

G000069065

Hexahedron

Hexa = 6

The hexahedron is usually called the cube. All six faces are squares and three of them meet at every vertex.

Octahedron

Octa = 8

All eight faces of the octahedron are equilateral triangles and four of them meet at every vertex.

Hexahedron

Coxeter's Symbol = (4,3)
Faces: 6
Vertices: 8
Edges: 12

Euler's Theorem
F + V = E + 2
6 + 8 = 12 + 2

Dual Figure: Octahedron

Dihedral Angle = 90°
Edge Angle = 90°
Angular Defect = 90°

A

D

D

D

B

D

C

C

C

A

Octahedron

Coxeter's Symbol = (3,4)
Faces: 8
Vertices: 6
Edges: 12

Euler's Theorem
F + V = E + 2
8 + 6 = 12 + 2

Dual Figure: Cube

Dihedral Angle = 109°28'
Edge Angle = 90°
Angular Defect = 120°

B

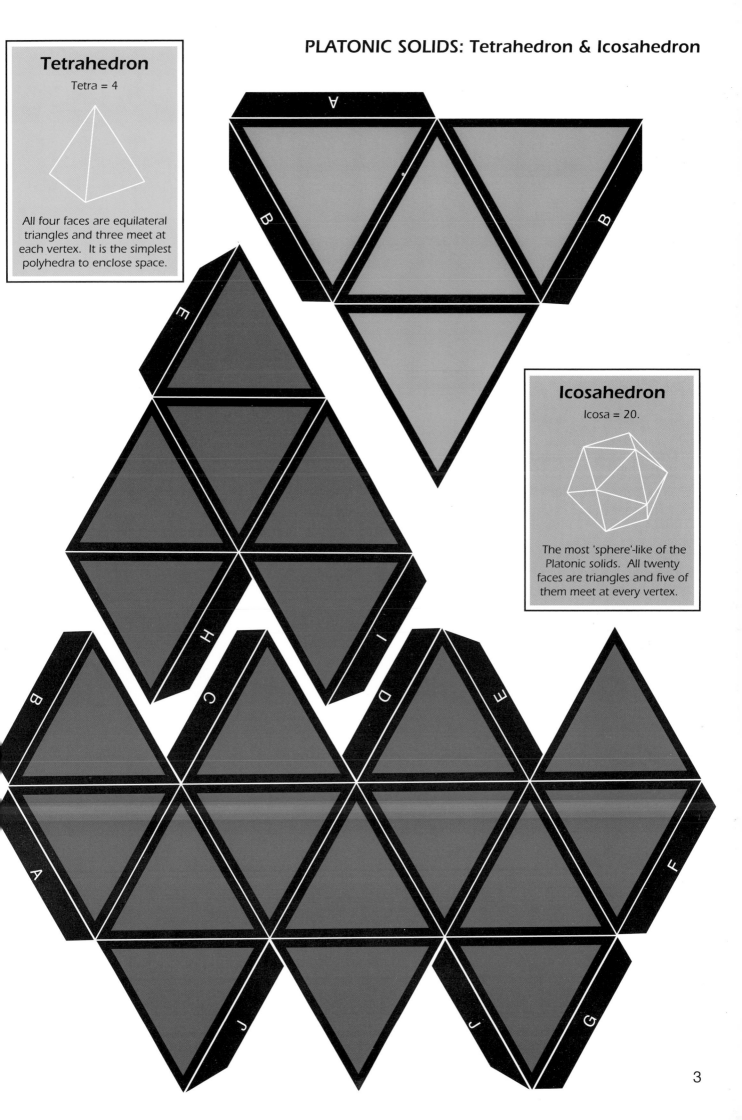

Tetrahedron

Tetra = 4

All four faces are equilateral triangles and three meet at each vertex. It is the simplest polyhedra to enclose space.

Icosahedron

Icosa = 20.

The most 'sphere'-like of the Platonic solids. All twenty faces are triangles and five of them meet at every vertex.

3

A

Tetrahedron

Coxeter's Symbol = (3,3)
Faces: 4
Vertices: 4
Edges: 6

Euler's Theorem
$F + V = E + 2$
$4 + 4 = 6 + 2$

Dual Figure: Self-dual

Dihedral Angle = 70°32'
Edge Angle = 109°28'
Angular Defect = 180°

B

B

B

Icosahedron

Coxeter's Symbol = (3,5)
Faces: 20
Vertices: 12
Edges: 30

Euler's Theorem
$F + V = E + 2$
$20 + 12 = 30 + 2$

Dual Figure: Dodecahedron

Dihedral Angle = 138°11'
Edge Angle = 63°26'
Angular Defect = 60°

A

F

H

G

E

E

D

C

J

J

I

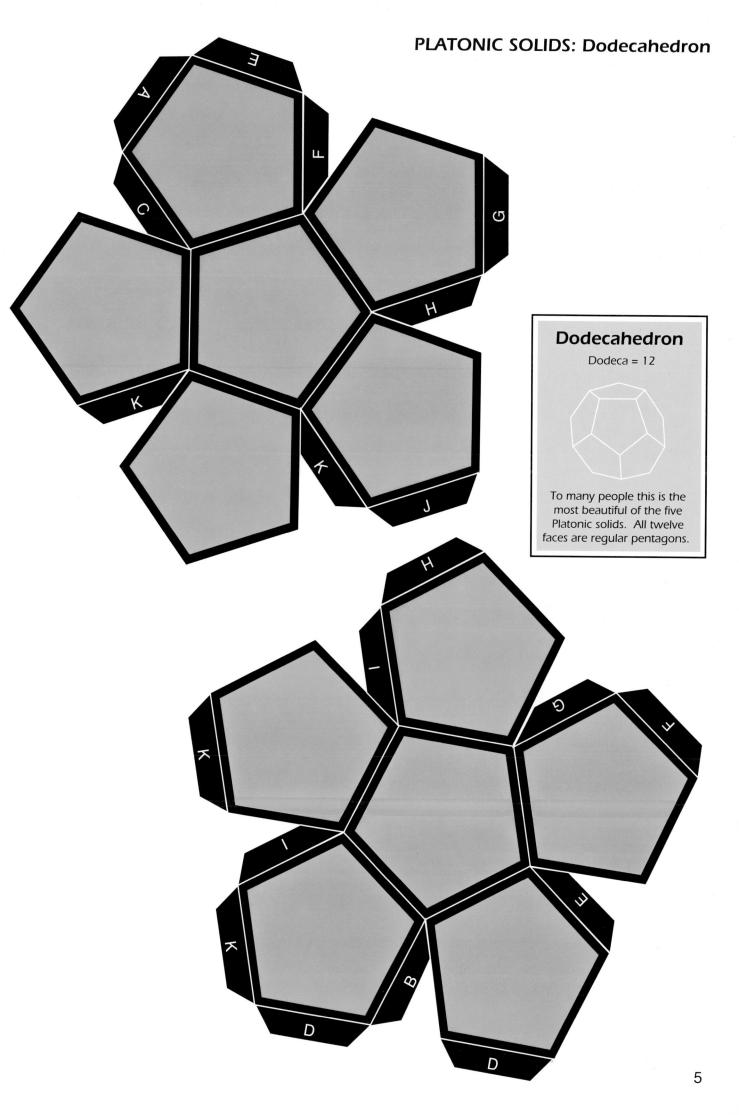

Dodecahedron

Dodeca = 12

To many people this is the most beautiful of the five Platonic solids. All twelve faces are regular pentagons.

Dodecahedron

Coxeter's Symbol = (5,3)
Faces: 12
Vertices: 20
Edges: 30

Euler's Theorem
F + V = E + 2
12 + 20 = 30 + 2

Dual Figure: Icosahedron

Dihedral Angle = 116°34'
Edge Angle = 41°49'
Angular Defect = 36°

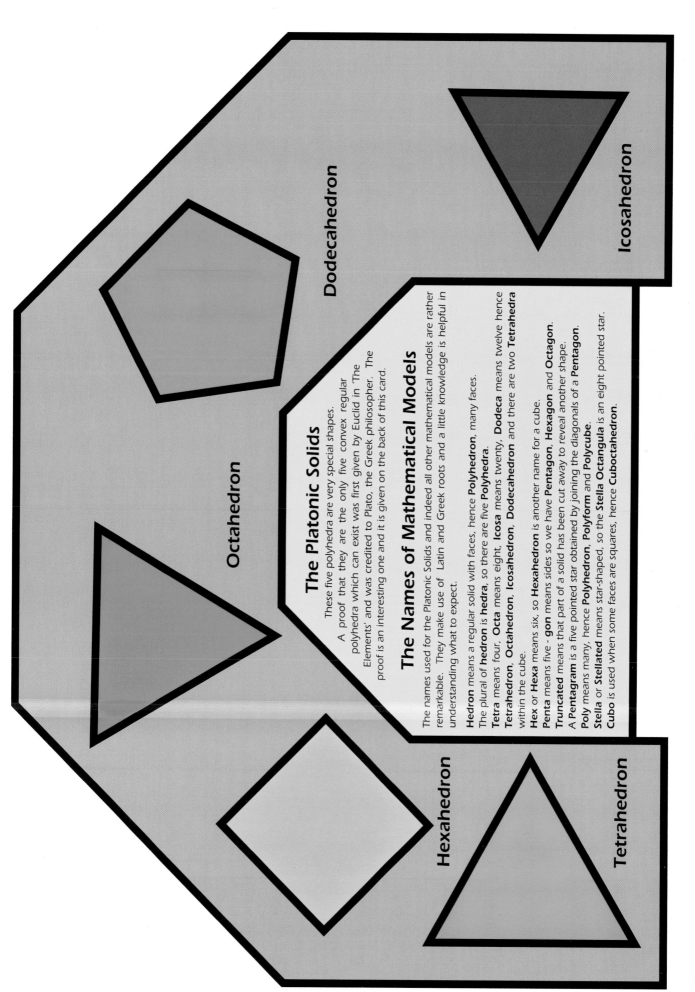

Icosahedron

Dodecahedron

Octahedron

Hexahedron

Tetrahedron

The Platonic Solids

These five polyhedra are very special shapes.

A proof that they are the only five convex regular polyhedra which can exist was first given by Euclid in 'The Elements' and was credited to Plato, the Greek philosopher. The proof is an interesting one and it is given on the back of this card.

The Names of Mathematical Models

The names used for the Platonic Solids and indeed all other mathematical models are rather remarkable. They make use of Latin and Greek roots and a little knowledge is helpful in understanding what to expect.

Hedron means a regular solid with faces, hence **Polyhedron**, many faces.
The plural of **hedron** is **hedra**, so there are five **Polyhedra**.
Tetra means four, **Octa** means eight, **Icosa** means twenty, **Dodeca** means twelve hence **Tetrahedron**, **Octahedron**, **Icosahedron**, **Dodecahedron** and there are two **Tetrahedra** within the cube.
Hex or **Hexa** means six, so **Hexahedron** is another name for a cube.
Penta means five - **gon** means sides so we have **Pentagon**, **Hexagon** and **Octagon**.
Truncated means that part of a solid has been cut away to reveal another shape.
A **Pentagram** is a five pointed star obtained by joining the diagonals of a **Pentagon**.
Poly means many, hence **Polyhedron**, **Polyform** and **Polycube**.
Stella or **Stellated** means star-shaped, so the **Stella Octangula** is an eight pointed star.
Cubo is used when some faces are squares, hence **Cuboctahedron**.

The Classic Proof

Two faces of a polyhedron must meet to create an edge and at least three faces and three edges are needed to create a vertex. At any vertex, the sum of the angles of the polygons meeting there must always be less than 360°. If the sum was 360°, then the vertex would be flat. If the sum was greater, then the vertex would not be convex. We can use this fact to see what regular polyhedra are possible. The faces must be regular polygons and their interior angles are as follows: triangle (60°), square (90°), pentagon (108°), hexagon (120°), heptagon (128.3°), octagon (135°) and so on.

If three triangular faces meet at a vertex, then the sum of their angles is 180° and the resulting polyhedron is the tetrahedron. If four triangular faces meet at a vertex then the sum is 240° and the resulting polyhedron is the octahedron. If five triangular faces meet at a vertex then the sum is 300° and the resulting polyhedron is the icosahedron. Six faces would give 360° and be flat, so no polyhedron is possible. Now try the square. Three squares give 270° and the cube. Four squares give 360° and no polyhedron. Now try the pentagon. Three pentagons give 324° and the dodecahedron. Four pentagons are not possible. Likewise three hexagons are already 360° and three heptagons, octagons or anything greater would already be too large.

Hence we can deduce that the five regular solids: the tetrahedron, the octahedron, the cube, the dodecahedron and the icosahedron are the only ones that can exist.

The Dictionary of Terms

Coxeter's Symbol: This is a numerical way of describing polyhedra which was devised by the mathematician H.S.M. Coxeter. It uses a pair of numbers within a bracket (x, y) where x is the number of sides the polygon faces have and y is the number of faces which meet at a vertex. Hence the symbol (4, 3) means that three square faces meet at each vertex. The polyhedron is a cube.

Euler's Theorem: Although this formula is only given for the Platonic Solids, it is true for all polyhedra which can be transformed into a sphere by topological transformation. It connects the numbers of faces, edges and vertices.

$$\text{Faces} + \text{Vertices} = \text{Edges} + 2$$

Dual Figures: These are pairs of polyhedra which are strongly related by each having the same number of faces as the other has vertices. An example of a dual pair is the Cube and the Octahedron. Another pair is the Dodecahedron and the Icosahedron. The tetrahedron has the same number of faces as edges and is therefore self-dual. Combinations of dual figures make interesting models and two have been included in this collection.

Dihedral Angle: The angle between two planes which meet to form an edge. It is the angle between lines in each of the planes which are at right angles to the edge that they share.

Edge Angle: The angle subtended by each edge at the centre of the sphere which passes through all the vertices of the polyhedron. This is called the circumscribing sphere.

Angular Defect: The angular defect is the angle by which the sum of the angles at the vertex falls short of 360°. There is a theorem, first proved by Descartes which states that the sum of the angular defects at all the vertices of any convex polyhedron is always 720°. Since all the vertices of each of the Platonic Solids are the same, it is easy to see how many vertices there must be.

Tetrahedron (720/180 = 4)
Octahedron (720/120 = 6)
Hexahedron (720/90 = 8)
Icosahedron (720/ 60 = 20)
Dodecahedron (720/24 = 30)

MODEL 6: Edge Dodecahedron

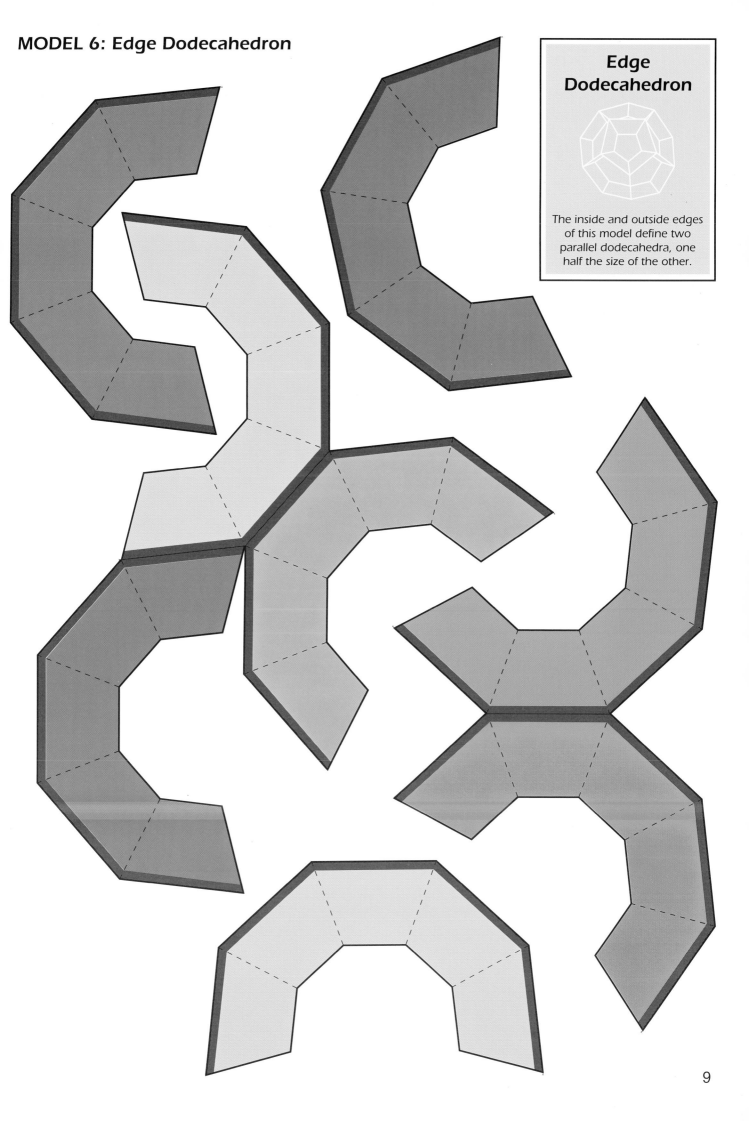

Edge Dodecahedron

An interesting feature of this model is that it requires no additional flaps to glue it together. Although the model is substantially hollow, the colour on the back of the sheet never shows. This shape was created by considering the dodecahedron as made of twelve equal pyramids sharing the same vertex and then bisecting their sloping edges.

18

10

17

14

22

5

18

6

20

16

19

8

8

14

2

10

1

13

2

17

1

3

25

13

4

11

12

30

11

15

24

12

3

26

27

15

24

23

25

22

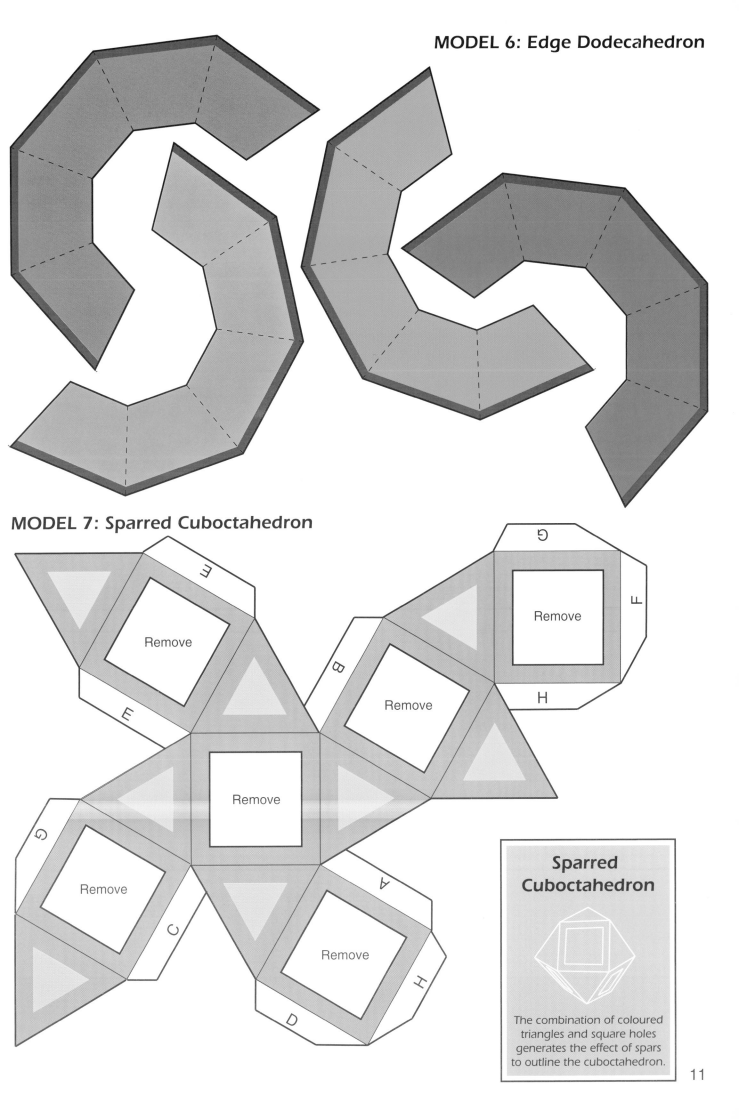

MODEL 6: Edge Dodecahedron

MODEL 7: Sparred Cuboctahedron

Sparred Cuboctahedron

The combination of coloured triangles and square holes generates the effect of spars to outline the cuboctahedron.

11

16

9/

7

21

27

19

26

19

7

28

29

28

6/

5

4

23

29

20

21

30

G

E

G

B

E

H

H

A

Sparred Cuboctahedron

The cuboctahedron is one of the 'Archimedian' polyhedra where the same numbers of two kinds of face meet at each vertex. In addition, each kind of face is entirely surrounded by the other. It can be obtained by truncating or slicing off the vertices of either an octahedron or a cube and so its name relates to both. It forms the basis for several of the models in this collection.

C

F

D

MODEL 8: Truncated Tetrahedron

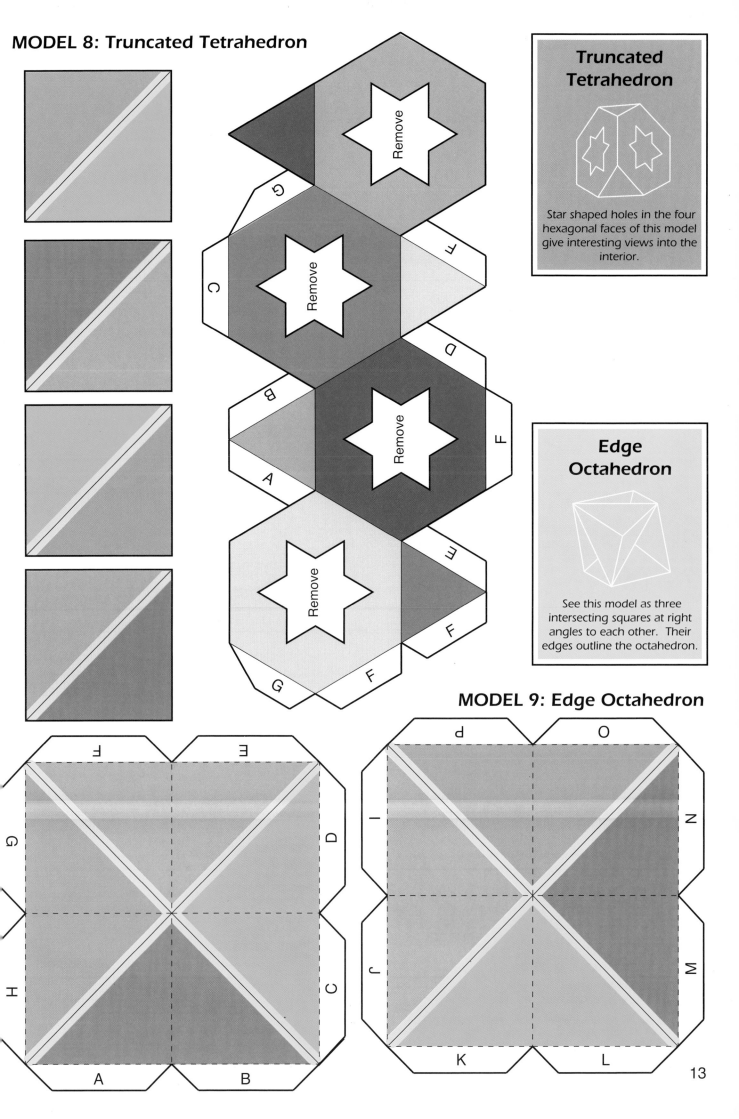

Remove

Remove

Remove

Remove

G

C

B

A

F

D

F

E

F

F

G

MODEL 9: Edge Octahedron

F

E

G

D

H

C

A

B

P

O

I

N

J

M

K

L

13

Truncated Tetrahedron

This model is also one of the facially regular 'Archimedian' polyhedra. Two regular hexagons and an equilateral triangle meet at every vertex. The six-pointed star holes are also interesting. They are made from two overlapping triangles of the same size as the triangular faces and the total area of the holes is equal to the area of one of the hexagonal faces.

Edge Octahedron

The broad yellow outline traces out the edges of the octahedron and the colouring scheme illustrates a way of looking at this model which ignores the three intersecting squares. There are eight dimples, two in each of four colours and the clockwise and anticlockwise sequences of those four colours meeting at a vertex includes all the possible permutations.

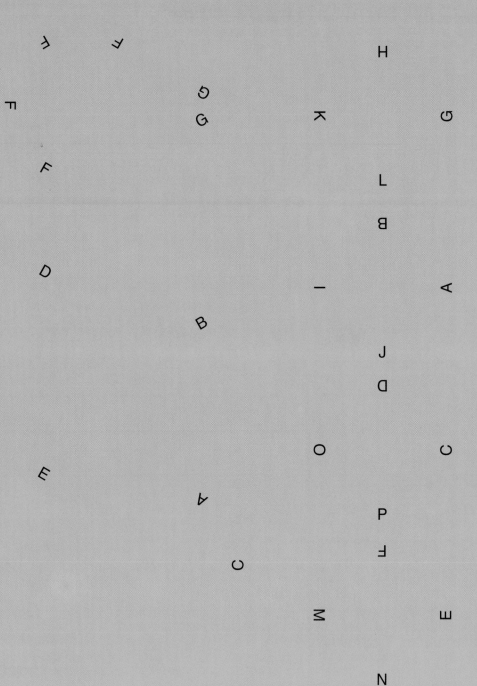

MODEL 10: Spiky Cuboctahedron

15

Spiky Cuboctahedron

The triangular faces of the underlying cuboctahedron have been extended outwards as triangular prisms until their sides have become squares. This means that each original square is now surrounded by four others. Note how the three colours on the sides of the prism alternate in clockwise and anticlockwise order around neighbouring spikes.

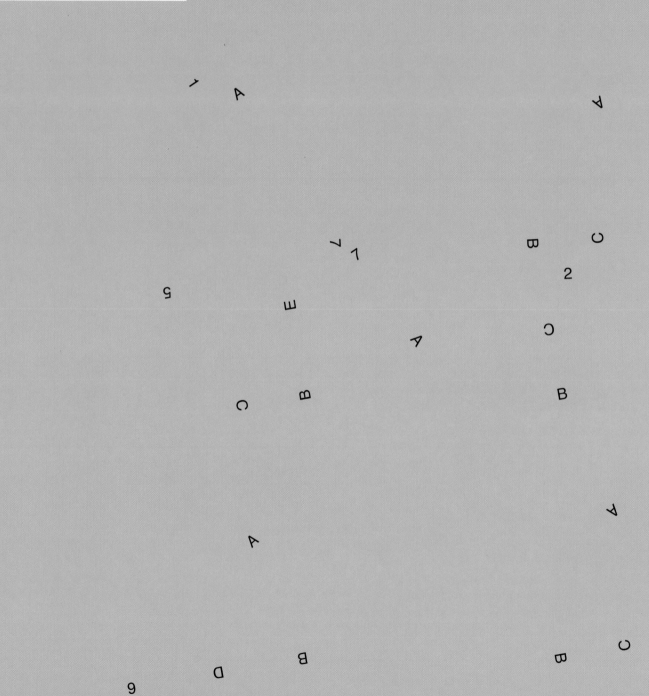

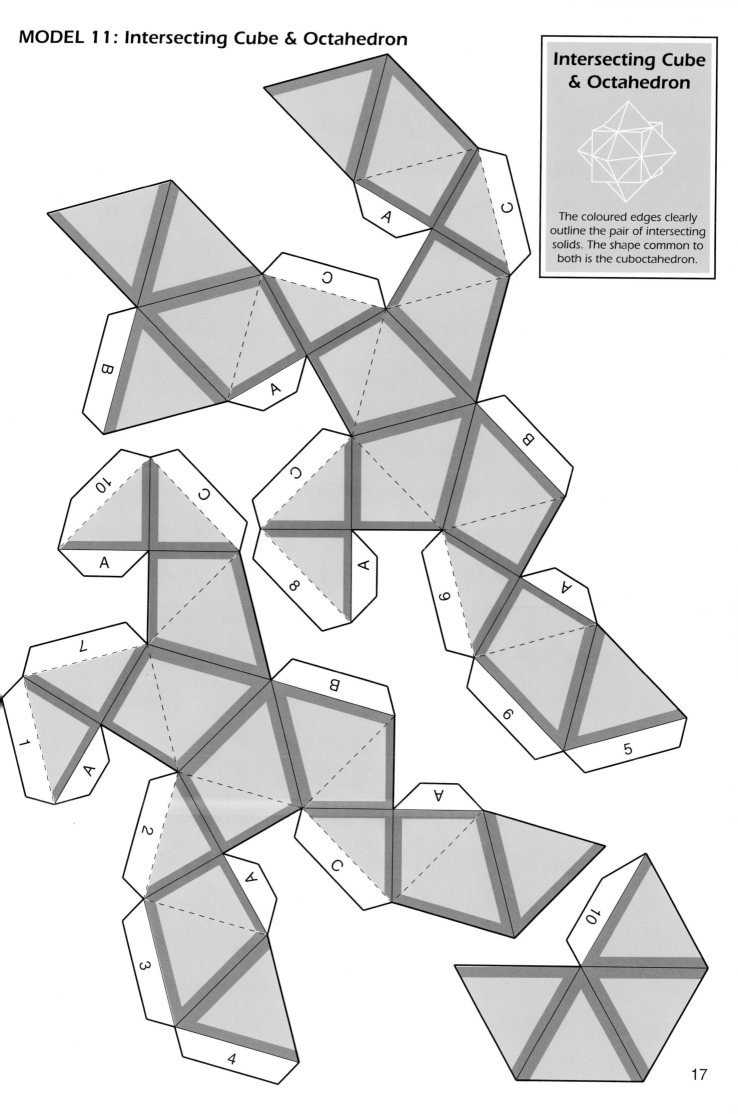

Intersecting Cube & Octahedron

The coloured edges clearly outline the pair of intersecting solids. The shape common to both is the cuboctahedron.

Intersecting Cube & Octahedron

An octahedron has 8 faces and 6 vertices and a cube has 6 faces and 8 vertices. Since they are dual figures each passes through all the mid-points of the edges of the other. In addition, if the neighbouring vertices are joined the resulting solid has 20 rhombic faces. It is a rhombic icosahedron. Cutting off all the protruding pyramids produces the underlying cuboctahedron.

3

A

C

A

1

2

B

A

B

A

C

A

B

A

C

A

A

A

A

C

C

9

5

V

10

10

8

C

18

9

MODEL 12: Edge Cuboctahedron

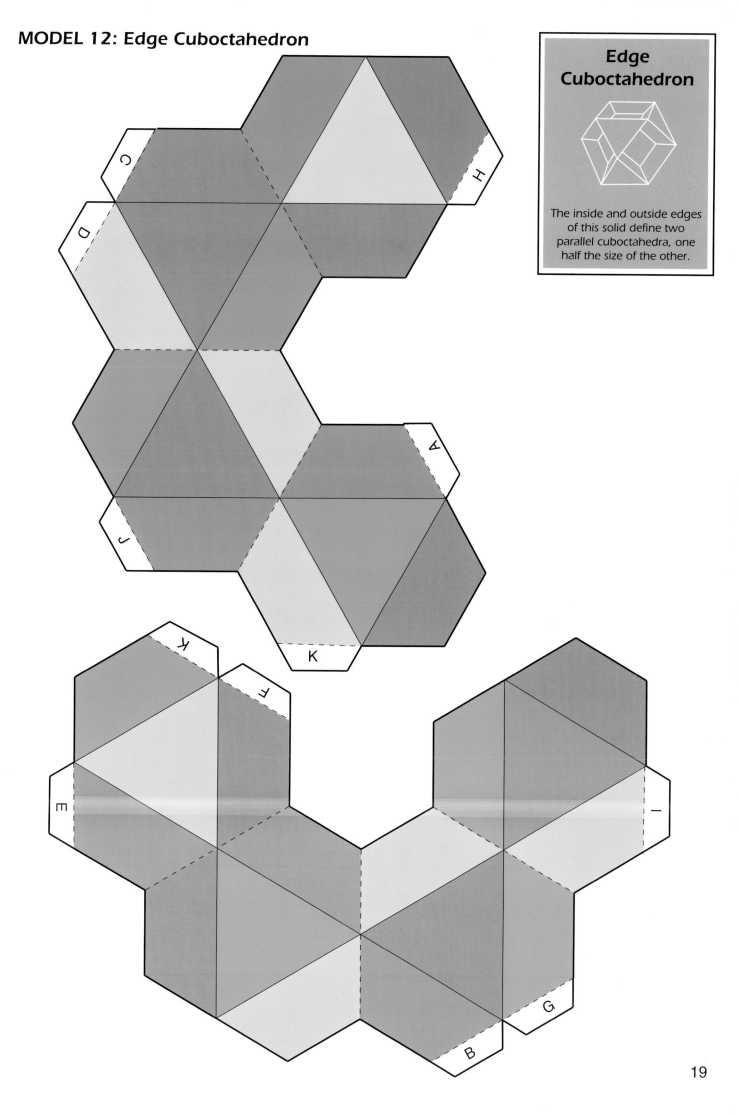

Edge Cuboctahedron

The inside and outside edges of this solid define two parallel cuboctahedra, one half the size of the other.

Edge Cuboctahedron

The cuboctahedron can be regarded as a group of touching pyramids with square and triangular bases. Each edge subtends an angle of 90° at the centre. To produce this model, the triangular faces have been left intact but the square faces have been inset to form hollow pyramids. Bisecting their sloping edges created a half-size hollow cuboctahedron at the centre.

G

B

A

E

H

I

K

F

K

J

D

C

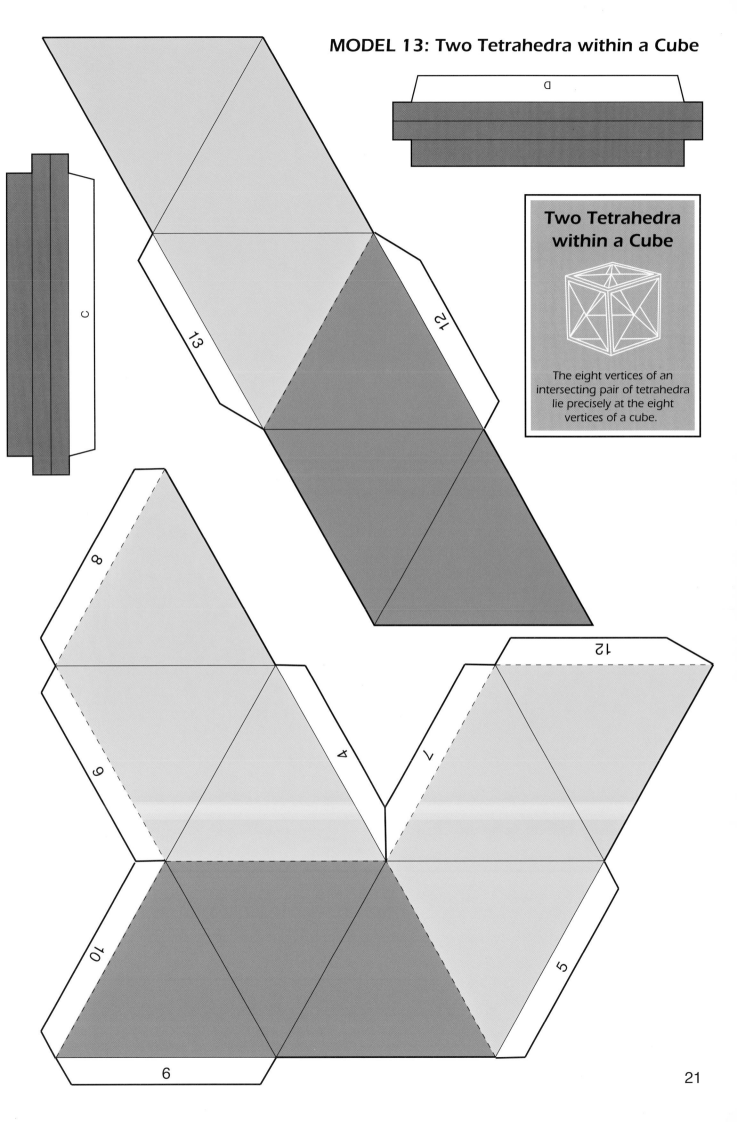

Two Tetrahedra within a Cube

The eight vertices of an intersecting pair of tetrahedra lie precisely at the eight vertices of a cube.

Two Tetrahedra within a Cube

A tetrahedron has four faces and four edges and so it is self- dual. This means that two tetrahedra will pass through each other in a completely symmetrical way to form a combination which is known as the 'Stella Octangula'. Not only do its eight vertices correspond to the eight vertices of the cube but its twelve edges are the twelve diagonals of the faces of the cube.

D

* *

13

10

13

* *

C

* *

11

12

4

12

5

6

13

MODEL 13: Two Tetrahedra within a Cube

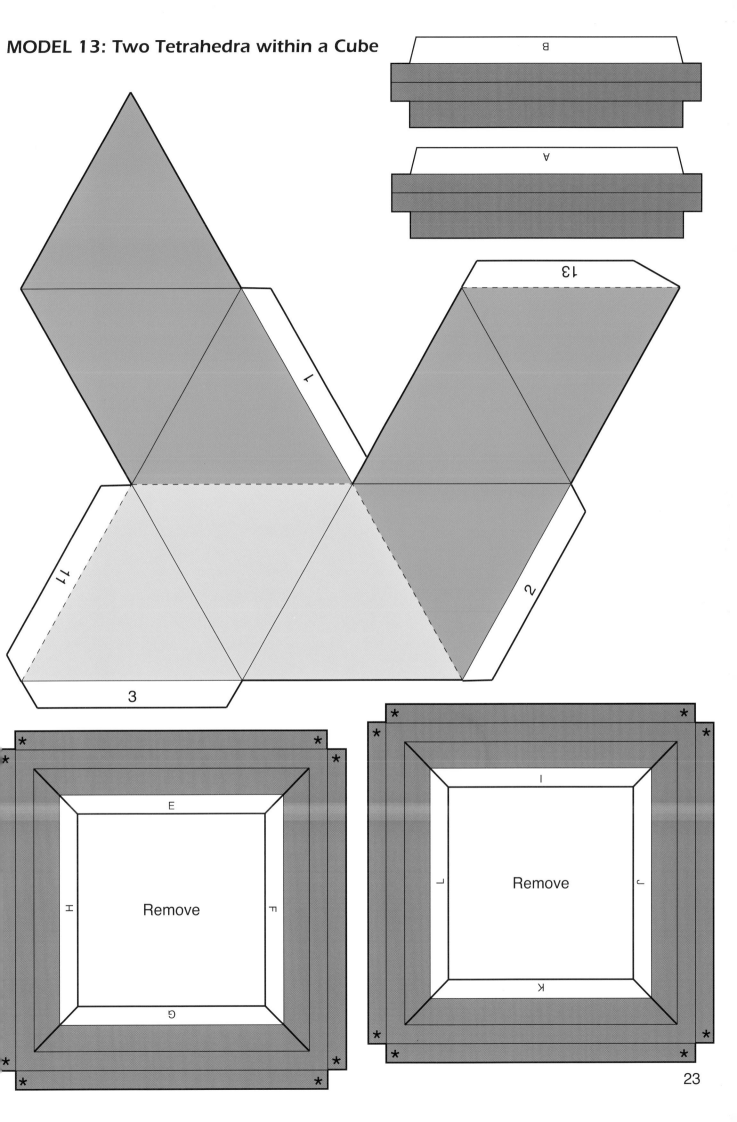

* *
* *

* *
* *

B

A

1

8

2

6

7

3

I

E

J

1

F

H

24

K

G

MODEL 14: Pentagram Polyhedron

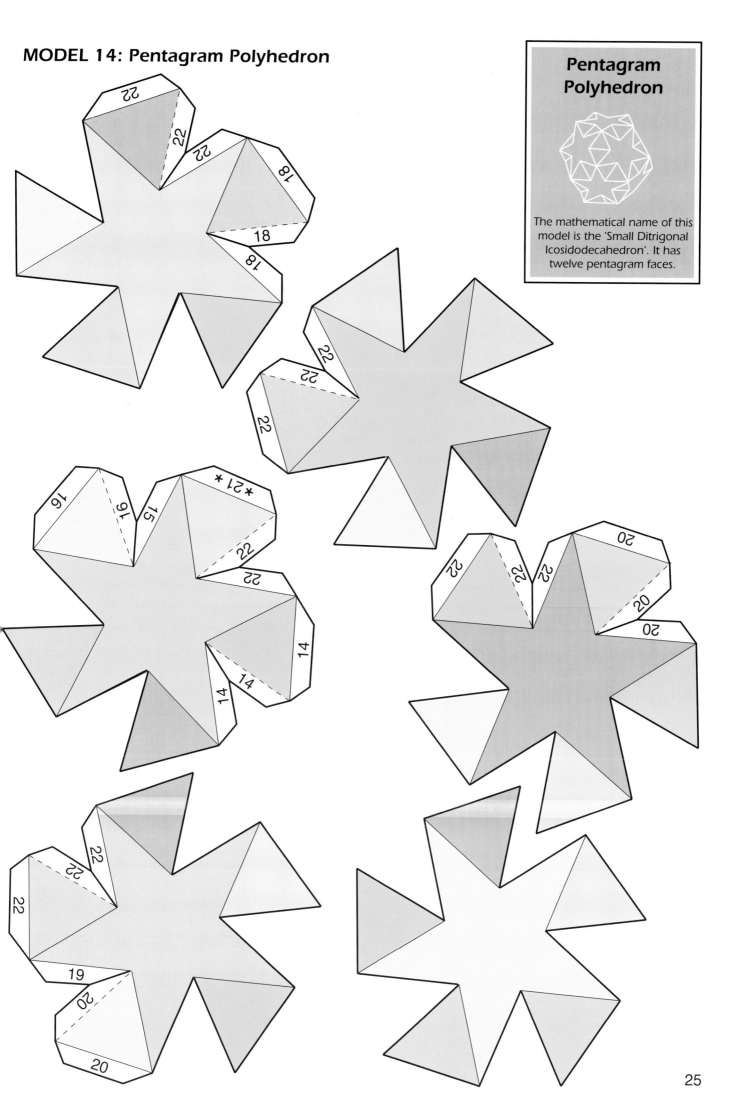

The mathematical name of this model is the 'Small Ditrigonal Icosidodecahedron'. It has twelve pentagram faces.

25

Pentagram Polyhedron

Pentagrams are obtained from the diagonals of a pentagon, so it is not surprising that their points lie at the vertices of a dodecahedron. The other faces are equilateral triangles and there are sixty of them. In all, there are twenty vertices where all six colours meet, three colours on the pentagrams and three on the triangles. Pentagrams of the same colour are always parallel.

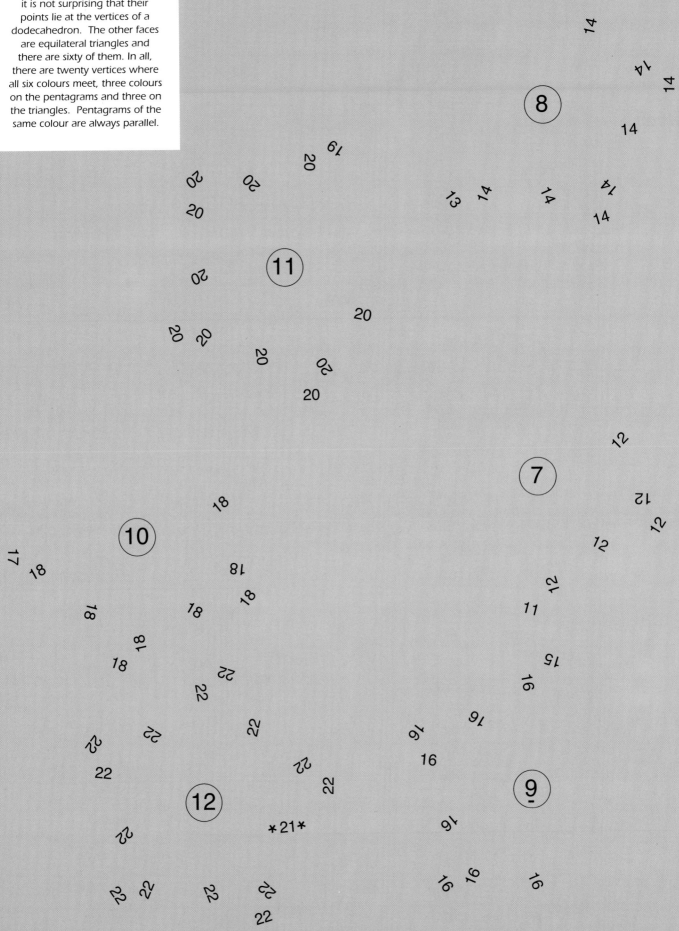

27

(1)

5

6

6

6

(4)

6

6

3

4

4

2

4

(3)

2

4

1

(2)

8

8

10

10

8

10

8

10

8

(5)

10

7

10

(6)

10

10

MODEL 15: Polycube

29

Polycube

This pleasantly jagged model is regular in the sense that all its faces are the same and there is a high degree of symmetry. However, three faces meet at some vertices and six at others and so it cannot be regarded as a regular polyhedron in the mathematical sense. However it retains the symmetry of the cube and larger members of the polycube family could be made.

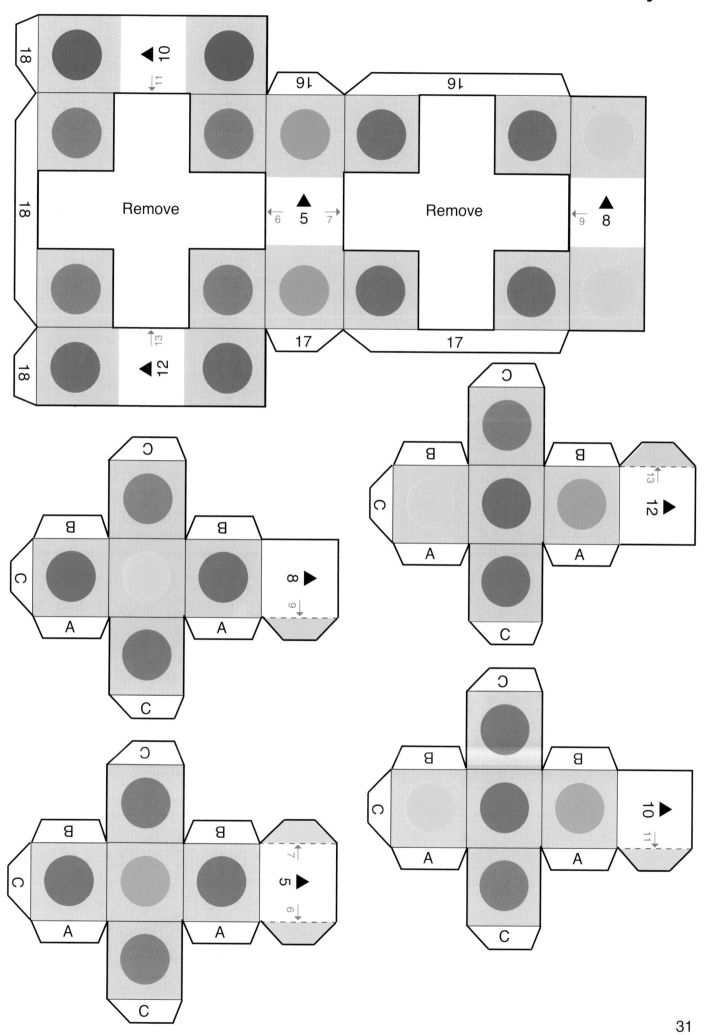

16

16

2

18

14 1   2 14   15 3   4 15
1   2   3   4

4

18   1   2   3   4 15
14 1   2 14   15 3   4

18   2   17

17

B B   B B

13
C
C
C   C
C
A A   C
C
9

A A

B B   B B

C
C   7
C   B B
11   C
C
A A   C
C
6
A A